black frag/ments

black frag/ments

Lolita Stewart-White

HUB CITY PRESS
SPARTANBURG, SC

Executive Director, Publisher: Meg Reid
Managing Editor: Kate McMullen
Marketing Assistant: Julie Jarema
Editor: Katherine Webb-Hehn
Poetry Series Editor: Jae Nichelle
Editor-at-large: Ashley M. Jones

Cover design: Chris Watts
Author Photo: Lolita Stewart-White

Type: Bell MT
Display: Naiche

Library of Congress Cataloging-in-Publication data has been applied for.

HUB CITY PRESS
153 N Spring Street
Spartanburg, SC 29306
1.864.577.9349

This book is dedicated to
Reginald B. White, my love and warrior.
And to Lola Reje White, my daughter—
my light—my everything.
I love you both tremendously!

table of contents

i see myself thrown heart first into this ruin

not for any crime
but being

> *"American Sonnet 2"*
> *Wanda Coleman*

African Americans have the highest death rate and shortest survival of any racial/ethnic group for most cancers. African American men also have the highest cancer incidence.

> *American Cancer Society*

Prelude to Blue

This be Middle Passage,
his frail body: a battered boat.
Must I sing my warrior an elegy?

Glory— glory— glory be—
thick with burden
when the enemy
colonizes his territory.

Burnt-Orange Mountain

The doctors say
there's a mountain

between your stomach
and esophagus

They tell me
the area's blocked

and that's why
you can't swallow

the spit
I crave

when you jam
your wet tongue

inside me
searching for treasures

The tumor's
described as malignant

A burnt-orange mountain
that might take you out

The doctors whisper
but all I hear

is the mountain's howl
I grab your frail fingers

strap on my boots
and climb

After the Diagnosis

No one smoothes out

my dark creases

unfolds my Mississippi

Goddam
in/vi/si/ble
dis/po/sa/ble

erased in

~~white~~

space

Damn Damn Damn

If god damn cancer

kills my husband

I am blackness
alone
on the plantation,
dark body contorted.
See the areola
lodged
in Miss Ann's
infant's mouth,
how far the nipple
stretches
across generations.
See the heart
buckle
bend will
to whiteness.

Good Times (Strange Fruit Episode, 1976)

Norman Lear has sent out a lynching invitation
to the nation – sent it out on the cover of a crumpled
TV Guide. The black father on Good Times must die.
Die because Norman Lear says he must.
The lynching takes place in a CBS studio.
The lynching airs prime time on Tuesday night.
I watch as if I'm at a wake – the linchpin
in my heart loosened. Remember the last scene?
How Florida Evans throws the punch bowl?
Black mother shattered / black father gone / black
family fragments / jagged glass on a project
apartment floor.

Damn

        Damn

                Damn

A Song for You

Come, my love. Drape your whiskey-colored skin
around my flesh, cape-like, so we can wear each other.
Bless me with the fullness of your body on the porch
of my imagination. Come, and I promise to touch you whole.
Please hurry, hurry, my love, before I am a field
of dead daffodils out yonder.

Kind of Blue: Variation One

Here, they tag the sick like oxen
and plod us down quiet corridors
to treatment rooms. I'm known
as patient #101 – a subject
tended like a field. Most days
my wife pushes me about because
I've lost what's left of my strength
and can barely stand. Here, I'm a slave
to their tonics. Here, I'm not a man.

Chorus of Ancestors

do no harm
to dark bodies
in ~~plantation's~~
hospital's
white walls
do no harm
to dark bodies
tethered
to infusion chairs
chained
to IV poles
do no harm
to dark bodies
shackled
to sickness
slave
to
massah's
medicines

FADE IN:

INT. EARLY MORNING – Camera pans to:

Shot of dark
girl in ~~white~~
space surrounded by
~~white~~ men in ~~white~~
coats surrounded
by perfect ~~white~~ teeth

surrounded by   explanation of
a black man's fate

Scene 1

Where are the cameras—the microphones?

I have forgotten to wear teal.
Why do these doctors speak down to me? (~~a chorus~~) (a mob)
Why do I listen? (~~an audience~~) (a shadow)
Where are the cameras—the microphones?
Why have I forgotten to wear teal?
When will these white men stop lecturing me? (~~a chorus~~) (a mob)
When will I allow myself to respond? (~~an audience~~) (a shadow)
Where are the cameras—the microphones?
Why have I forgotten to wear teal like Anita Hill?
Does whiteness remember I'm part of the discussion? (~~a chorus~~) (a mob)
Do I remember how to assert my blackness? (~~an audience~~) (a shadow)
Where are the cameras—the microphones?

Q&A

Wife's question:

Why won't you go to the doctor?

Husband's answer:

a) The doctor is no place for a black man.
b) The doctor is no place for a black man.
c) The doctor is no place for a black man.
d) The doctor is no place for a black man.

Wife's question:

Must the doctor mean pain?

Husband's answer:

Ask those brothas from Tuskegee how doctors ripped
open acres of their skin. How three fifths of their bodies
equaled human experiments. Ask how doctors ignored
the Nuremburg code, dissected Negroes' darkness
in search of Dinknesh in their bones

African ~~American~~ Sentence

Fear
of
white
men
in
white
coats
who
police
dark
bodies
with
stethoscopes

Exhibit A: Tuskegee Experiment

FADE IN:

History's microphone looms in a ~~white~~
sterile room.
Dr. Taliaferro Clark clears his throat coated with
the scent of bad blood.

"Mason County is a natural laboratory,
a ready-made situation. The rather low
intelligence of the Negro population, depressed
economic conditions, and the very common
promiscuous relations not only contribute
to the spread of syphilis but to the prevailing
indifference with regard to treatment."

Free Blood Test.
Free Treatment
By County Health
Department and
Government Doctors:
YOU MAY FEEL
WELL AND STILL
HAVE BAD BLOOD
COME AND BRING
ALL YOUR FAMILY.

Bad blood	Colored-County	
Backwoods	A / la / bam / a	Sharecroppers
(un)refined	(un)beloved	(un)examined
(un)touchable	(un)cultivated	(un)wanted
(un)desirable	(un)suspecting	(un)protected
(un)kempt	(un)done	(un)moored

The House that was my Husband's Body

has collapsed &
I stand alone
teetering on his
broken steps.
There is no mahogany door.
No brass doorknob
for my smooth-brown
hand to turn. No reveille
to awaken him
like Colored troops
in 1863 when they swallowed
their first good taste
of freedom
& marched about town
clutching the promise
of Proclamation
in their dirt-stained hands
the way I find myself
clutching the notion
of my husband's
reconstruction.

Kind of Blue: Variation Two

Again, these damn doctors ask to weigh me.
Don't they know the scale is a fortune teller,
its numbers my enemy? Don't they see my wife
in the background pretending? Her eyes seem
distracted, but I know differently. I can feel
her brown irises – the cuts of them – wound me.
What has happened to the man I was – the mass
that could fill these sagging jeans?

Dear Wife,

More than anything else in my world; thoughts
of you cross my mind all the time. Some are trying;
some are helpful; some hurt and some feel good.
But you know all of them put together don't come close
to the one feeling that will never change: I love you!
It's the best one of all.

Happy 2nd Anniversary

Love, R

Reconstruction

The surgeon explains

how he'll chip away

the burnt-orange

mountain that glistens

inside my husband's throat

like history's shame

then

patch

his

blackness

until

he is

14th amendment

sturdy

and

guaranteed

what?

Way in the Middle of the Air

Surgeon

Incisions carved in your abdomen

Your chest split

The tumor gutted

Part of the esophagus detached

The food pipe rebuilt

Reattached to your stomach

There are risks of complications

Husband

branding mama warned me about
where heat strikes   ignites flesh into flame
third-degree scarred nigger remains
tunnel dimmed—where's the freedom train
tracks constructed from Harriet's breath
greedy to cross the Mason-Dixon line
I just want to see how the chariot feels

fragment

(n.): 1. a small or broken part separated from something
as when a black ~~birch~~
is hacked by america's
ax / dark bark skinned /
limbs splintered /
massive trunk chopped
by the (un)relenting swing
of a steel blade

Our Daughter's Responses in a Counseling Session

Q: How's school?

A: Nobody notices me – hears me whisper for Daddy.

Q: How do you feel about your father being ill?

A: A little sad.

Q: Do you understand the nature of his illness?

A: Esophageal cancer.

Q: Tell me about your nightmares?

A: Daddy is dark.

Q: What would you do if you had a magic wand?

A: Make Daddy live forever like Harry Potter.

Q: Any anxiety?

A: Sometimes.

Q: Are you afraid?

A:

Dear Dad,

I hope you have a wonderful birthday. I love you very much and I am so happy you're my father. You are the best at making potatoes and macaroni.

Love, L

Text from a Friend

Tuesday, April 4, 3:30 p.m.

I'm not supposed to tell
you this, but G told me L
was sad today in school
because her dad is back
in the hospital. She said
she tried her best
to cheer her up. I thought
you should know.

Tuesday, April 4, 3:35 p.m.

Hi. Please tell G thank you
for being such a good
friend. We're on our way
to the hospital now to see
L's dad. I'll talk to her.

Text to self

Tuesday, April 4, 3:38 p.m.

How do I talk to her
with a fist   jammed
in my throat   knuckles
fracture   my alto.

Everything is a Black Girl

Yellow
light
floods
his
hospital
room
&
our
daughter
becomes
a
Kara
Walker
silhouette
She sees what's left of her father and smoke rises
She sees what's left & her lynch braids ignite
She's a shadow burning.
A black girl's ashes.

Kind of Blue: Variation Three

Can someone tell me what fuels this hurt?
The devil dwells in my throat.
Fire & brimstone when I open my mouth.
Radiation burns my tongue,
darkens whiskey-colored skin.
Food = Heat = Holler
Who struck the match,
set my insides ablaze like kindling?

Heartache Ghazal

My whiskey-colored man be Billie's bruised throat.
Lonely blue note hung up in her throat.

My whiskey-colored man be bluesy,
Sunday gloomy, raspy like Lady Day's throat.

In the evenings, he be fine & mellow. Smooth—
as whiskey soothing a dark woman's throat.

Some nights his whiskey-colored hands hold me tight
when a blue moon swells in the sky's sweet throat.

When my whiskey-colored man loves me
just right, broken notes scatter from my throat.

By sunrise, my whiskey-colored man be a ghost.
Good Morning Heartache echoes in my throat.

Afro Beautiful

circa back in the day

We cuddle

in a breakfast joint.

Our desire

simmers

like fish & grits.

I gaze at his full lips.

He blows the

black

in his coffee & sips.

I swear this yellow boy

be Afro beau /

ti /

ful

My heart be the steam

in his cup.

Definition of Blue

dysphagia (n.). 1. difficulty in swallowing / when food or water goes down the throat the wrong way and rushes out / like steaming summers when b-boys pried open a red hydrant's mouth and water spat onto pavement. 2. a symptom of disease associated with pain and discomfort esp. the first time you cough up sips of water / drops that won't go down / your throat gags and trembles / I watch you choke.

Oncology Elegy

The white oncologist widens my third eye
with *if*
    with *maybe*
        with *could be*
            with *pet/scan*
              with *tumor*

within *24 hours*   we'll know

The white oncologist snatches out my heart
    squeezes it tight
like the knot
on Aunt Jemima's headscarf
with *mammy*

with *will I be a widow?*

Chorus of Ancestors

our brotha cries out
and we come   armed:
slick with prayer
                    oil
hoodoo
        voodoo
everlasting holy
sun-blessed fists
                        clenched
with spells
     & magic healing
sage burning palms
spiritual napalm
                        cast
          demons out
anointed tongues
sharp as machetes
                        swinging
in cane fields

How to Shield a Dark Body

I study the creases of my husband's dark body,
Dark body surgeons will dismantle come morning.

    There are countless ways to dismantle a dark body:
    scalpel – whistle – rope

A whistle floats across the sky and spooks the night.
At least that's the way my grandma likes to tell it.

    The way grandma tells the story of Emmett lingers.
    Scent loud like the smell of a wilted gardenia.

Come morning my husband may wilt like a gardenia.
I want to pluck him from this garden to protect him.

    I want to protect my husband but don't know how.
    Is there any way to shield a dark body from harm?

Emmett's mama couldn't shield his dark body from harm.
I study the creases of my husband's dark body.

Right On!

circa back in the day

When no one is looking
I lift my navy-blue blouse
and let my man kiss my navel
bury his pouty lips
inside my brown sun.
Yes Lord, I feel his warm
skin brush against my stomach.
His tongue hallelujah hot
as he takes in my heat and we

spark

Exhibit B: Billing Department

I'm escorted downstairs
        like Mama the day
she was banished
                to the basement
of Sears Department Store
        to try on spring dresses.

They wanted her birch-
brown body
        out of sight.

Can you see my blackness
alone in a corner office
where a white hospital clerk
        wears a smirk?

She says my husband's chemo
can't begin until I lay down
        some paper.

She says grants for his kind
        of cancer are unavailable
because it's not common
like breast or lung cancer.

What a pity I can't pay
        with the forty acres
and a mule owed to me
and my peeps.

Kind of Blue: Variation Four

My brown body
has been locked away
in a hospital room
like contraband. Nobody
hears my melody –
sees me flee these cold,
white walls, defiance
in my jaws, freedom
in my mouth,

O refuge,

O fugue,

O fugitive

blue.

Healing

Dear Diaspora:

I am black balm soothing

I am black balm soothing

I am black balm soothing

A smoke prayer

Burn of Amen in our throats

Bloodline dope like kin-

folk passed down

Thick of our loveliness

We are the ones we've been waiting for

Night has brought this offering

scent of his whiskey skin

My husband unfurls his Union Blue

I turn the cool side of my finger north

Fugitivity

I turn the cool side of
my finger north. Defiance
is a traveling pass
that glitters in my back pocket.
My skin drinks
the unfettered flame of first light.
I'm history's half shadow.
Half my lover's sway stashed
away in Freedman's Bank.

Our bodies r black refrains sucked
from the femur of Dinknesh. I glimpse
nappy speckles of ourselves.
We juba in the black
outdoors
unpen the night &
let our seams glimmer. We
don't need permission
to touch.

The House that was my Husband's Body

A shack,

a splintered door,

gray windows.

I stand alone teetering

on his broken porch.

Where's the tarnished knob

my brown hand turns?

Where's the hallway,

a speck of light

that leads to his parlor?

Can we dance tonight?

How do I steady

his fragile frame,

hold bones that loosen

like floorboards?

Husband's Instructions

Verse

1. *Do not resuscitate*

2. *Do not cremate*

3. *Do not bury me in a pale blue suit*

4. *Do not open the casket*
   like they did for that boy
   they found bruised-blue
   in the river

Chorus of Ancestors

"Oh Lord I want two wings"

"Oh Lord I want two wings"

"Oh Lord I want two wings"

" So the world can't do me no harm"

Instructions for Intimacy after your Partner's Cancer Treatment

Assume the dominant role during intercourse.
Beware of touch. Fingertips can leave

evidence, bruise whiskey-colored skin.
Try positions requiring less energy.

Avoid sex after a heavy meal.
For comfort, plan uninterrupted time.

Avoid extremes in temperatures.
Consider the hands – they must be supple

to unfold a wound. Dim the lights. Burn
candles. Make moves while your partner

remains a passive shadow. Tonight, I'll rub
against his velvet skin, the way I rub

the jagged C-section scar burning my belly
and pray and pray and pray he doesn't recoil.

Dear Death

Tell me how to (un)dress my blackness after the battle is over—

how to hold my worn hands steady to (un)do my fatigues

and boots, how to (un)fold my public face so my jawbone can slip

and fall. Tell me whose willing shoulder will wait?

fragment

(v.): 1. break or cause to break into fragments
as when a bruised black
~~birch~~ falls and lands
with a thud in a forest
of white ~~birch trees~~ and
nobody claims to hear it

Exhibit C: Henrietta Lacks Speaks

There is no escape—
my harvested cells held
in place on a microscopic stage,
shifted back & forth
in artificial light. Where is the sun?
How many arctic-blue eyes
have glanced into this instrument
for a chance to observe my DNA,
fulfill their curiosity, as if
they're at a peep show
and I'm their
Venus Hottentot
minus my body?
I never asked for immortality.

AFib (or Revolution Redux)

My heart has grown wings:
jagged rhythms
& thumps, the striking
of drums:
Doctors dart
about with Mason jars
but they can't catch my soul

brotha funk,
on beat one
throbbing heat,
that melts
their winter
& gives way to spring

Call and Response

Dear Mr. W:

Please consider giving
the gift of blood & tissue
samples during
your upcoming surgery.
Imagine the ~~white~~ people
you could help
with your donation.
Imagine how you
could advance our
medical research.

They want to scrape my blackness
into a petri dish, sample
its blood-beats & rhymes
synthesize a black man's holler
pluck darkness from my bassline
study how it fades
They want to rob
rasp from my throat   *mutate*
my notes like Henrietta's cells
decode

decode

decode

my Negro

Dear Husband:

I'm proud of you for so many things
Everyone has a hiding place, and you are mine.

You work so hard to make me strong
Everyone has a hiding place, and you are mine.

I love when your hands anoint my skin like prayer
Everyone has a hiding place, and you are mine.

I'm your queen all day, all night
Everyone has a hiding place, and you are mine.

Love L

Kind of Blue: Variation Five

The needle pierces the port inside my skin.
I breathe – sigh – take in my new lover
like wonder. The nurse points to the IV bag
and mouths Oxaliplatin. I close my eyes,
pretend my body isn't being poisoned.
Help. How do I make this go away?
How can I stop myself from crying out
for my wife to hold me? I didn't know
the body could be a stream to drown in.

How to Cry Without Tears

If the Cancer remains local—
        If the Cancer spreads to lymph nodes—
If the Cancer is treated with stem cells—
        If the Cancer is mastered by surgery—
If the Cancer colonizes your brown body—
        If the Cancer is (un)treatable—
If the doctors say—
        If the doctors say—
If the doctors say—

All we can do is make him comfortable
Suck
it
up
dark
girl
Suck
it
up
like
breath
Let
it
marinate
on
your
tongue
Bare your teeth
        & gums—
                scream out the notion of death!

Root of My Blues

My baby
is almost
gone
and I am
dark
alone

I say
my baby
is almost
gone
and how
do I
carry on

Our bed
is black
as death
and all
that's left
is blues
on my
breath

My baby
is almost
gone
and I am
dark
alone

Chorus of Ancestors

we do not consent
to the avalanche
of cracked ice
arctic-blue eyes
frosty faces that freeze
our brotha out
we do not consent
to winter's howl
how it growls
drowns our sistah's
summer brown
we do not consent
to this bitter blizzard
that buries a black
family's bones
beneath the heaviness
of snow

African ~~American~~ Sentence

Way
back
when
I'd
fling
open
my
husband's
doors
loot
and
plunder
for
love

Emanicipation Blues

Homeless (adj.): 1. of a person without a home. 2. Emancipated from the arms of my man who held me even when I was in my feelings. 3. This freedom hurts / like cracked hands aching for plots of (un)promised land / like a dark girl's midnight craving the moon.

The House that was my Husband's Body

brick   hurled
match   lit
flames   ablaze
husband's   body
burning   tenement:
slick   black-
berry   brick
scarred   charred
smoke   chokes

the
gorgeous
black
boy
in
him
like
Rodney
like
Eric
like
George

fragmented

(adj): 1. existing or functioning as though broken

into separate parts / disorganized /

disunified /

as when a black ~~birch tree~~

is uprooted

replanted

in troubled soil

god

knows

where

Exhibit D: Dem Dark Bones

America craves the taste of dark meat.
She licks glimmers of salt from burdened shoulders

Niggas shoulder the burden of Corona.
Niggas dying early ain't nothing new.

New word for dying is essential worker.
Essential is the sound of niggas' crushed bones.

America sucks our marrow bone dry.
America picks snowy teeth with dark bones.

Dem dark bones Ezekiel prophesized:
Rising up in the valley, dem dark bones.

Dem dark bones that helped build ~~white~~ America.
Why aren't dark bones considered American?

America considers dark bones her feast.
America craves the taste of dark meat.

And You Don't Stop

circa back in the day

my husband lifts me

on to his umber shoulders

boom-box high

to vibe with peeps

at a block party fish fry

where black pride am/pli/fies

and you don't stop   the static

e/lec/tro/mag/net/ic

~~radiation~~ radio

raheem joy

that won't be contained

freedom waves that vibrate

beyond an inner-

city sky

yo!

Prayer in A Minor

jesus, please, roll
away the stone
from his esophagus
like you rolled
the stone away
from lazarus's tomb
jesus heal him
bring him forth
from the cradle
of death's womb
please, jesus, speak
his beautiful name
call it out
like you called
out to lazarus
from the grave

Anointed

my husband's

long   muscular

arms yawn

 sun streams

  through arched

 fingers

body: a cathedral

ebony steeple

stretches over me

    sunday

    morning

    blessing

Chorus of Ancestors

resistance!
        resistance!
                resistance!
                        justice
                for the struggle
don't you remember
        the drums
throbbing tongues
thumping lungs
        bumping chests
    b
    o
    o
    m
    i
    n
    g
blooming (un)rest
blood
l
a
c
k
                protest

Kind of Blue: Variation Six

I'm a man, not property,

meaning no one owns me,

not the doctors who've shown me

the point of entry, where their scalpels

lay claim to impenetrable darkness.

I'm a man, not an object

to be dissected

            & reassembled at will.

I'm a man, not a boy,

who owes everything, owns nothing.

Reparations bloom in my bones.

Revolutionary Fragments

My husband's throat revolts
(un)swallows:

stings
      of tasers
blows
      of knuckles
strikes
      of billy clubs
blasts
      of shotguns
cracks
      of bullwhips
clinks
      of shackles

Can you smell rebellion?

Black as Material, Mode and Movement

I'm black. Out
of fashion. Denimed
down in dark.
On me, America's
got papers. America's
got papers on me.

*

We render unruly.
Resist! Resist!
with the funk
of our utterances.
In the mode of indigo
we get down!
We get down
in the mode of indigo!

*

By the rusted washtub,
we syncopate
our ancestors' ache.
We be lit
by the gospel of night!
We got bars!
You can't burn beautiful.

Intensive Care Rebellion

I'm planted

in my husband's hospital room

like the American flag

Crispus Attucks fought for.

Look into my eyes!

Dark stars illuminate a midnight

ache that reverberates

across my warrior's landscape. Damn!

My blackness glitters,

full citizenship on display. I demand

my husband be healed!

Sweet shade of a brown boy returned to me.

He won't be a casualty,

like Attucks splattered in blood.

Self-Portrait as Hoodie

black
woman
be
hoodie
hovering
ovah
what
remains
of
her
husband's
woolly
mane
she
be
angel
of
fleece
kissing
his
scalp
golden
she
be
blockin'
blows

with
crushed
softness
she
be
darkness
clinging
to
his
skin
she   be black   ten/ der/ ness   lingering

Sounder, 1972

Praise sweet
          Nathan-Lee
how he grips
          a make-shift crutch
under the crease
          of his armpit
& hobbles

                              Praise Rebecca's
                                        bare-feet how
                              they hasten
                                        down a dirt road
                                        running
                                                  running
                                                            desperately

Praise motion
          how it propels
these lovers forward
          faster &
                    faster
until their blackness
          blurs

                              Praise the gaze
                                        of a dark girl
                              mesmerized in a theater
                                        by the notion of black love
                                        how hands glimmer
                                        when they embrace

Notes

"After the Diagnosis" borrows the line "Mississippi Goddam" from Nina Simone's song, of the same name, which appeared on the album, *Nina Simone in Concert*, 1964.

"Good Times (or Strange Fruit Episode, 1976)" is based on the television show, *Good Times* episode, "The Big Move," when James Evans, Sr. dies in a car crash.

"A Song for You" borrows its title from Donny Hathaway's ballad of the same name, which appeared on the album, *Donny Hathaway*, 1971.

"Kind of Blue" borrows its title from Miles Davis's album of the same name.

"FADE IN:" mentions Anita Hill, an American lawyer, educator and author, who burst onto the national scene when she accused U.S. Supreme Court nominee, Clarence Thomas, her supervisor at the United States Department of Education and Equal Employment Opportunity Commission of sexual harassment.

In "Q & A," The word Dinknesh means you are marvelous in Amharic. It was the name given to the 3.2-million-year-old fossilized skeleton discovered in Ethiopia in 1974.

"Exhibit A: Tuskegee Experiment" was a study conducted between 1932 and 1972 by the United States Public Health Service and the Centers for Disease Control and Prevention on a group of African American men with syphilis and a control group without. Dr. Taliaferro Clark, lead physician of the venereal disease division, played a key role in initiating the study to observe the effects of the disease when left untreated.

"Way in the Middle of the Air" borrows its title from a line in the spiritual, "Ezekiel Saw De Wheel". The line, "I just want to see how the chariot feels," was taken from the African American spiritual, "Now Let Me Fly." The line, "... constructed from Harriet's breath," refers to abolitionist and social activist, Harriet Tubman.

"Everything is a Black Girl" borrows its title from an *Art-Biweekly* article about the contemporary artist Kara Walker. The poem was inspired by Walker's silhouette "Burn".

"Heartache Ghazal" was inspired by Billie Holiday's song, "Good Morning Heartache". The poem also references Holiday's songs: "Blue Moon" and "Fine and Mellow".

"Oncology Elegy" mentions Aunt Jemima, a character based on a minstrel show and linked to the "mammy" stereotype.

"How to Shield a Dark Body," a Duplex after the poet Jericho Brown makes mention of the name Emmett, which refers to Emmett Till, a 14-year-old, African American boy, who was abducted and killed in Money, Mississippi, in 1955, after being accused of whistling at a white woman.

"Exhibit B: Billing Department," mentions forty acres and a mule, which was a promise made during the Civil War that freed slaves would receive 40 acres of land and a mule. The promise was never fulfilled.

"Healing" borrows language from June Jordan's poem for "South African Women".

In "Fugitivity," The word juba is of African origin. It

refers to a dance that involves hand clapping and slapping. "Freedman's Bank," established by Congress in 1865, helped African Americans access capital after the Civil War.

"Instructions for Intimacy after your Partner's Cancer Treatment" borrows language from the Dana Farber Cancer Institute's website.

"Husband's Instructions" borrows language from the African American spiritual "Two Wings".

"Exhibit C: Henrietta Lacks Speaks" is about Henrietta Lacks, an African American mother of five, whose cells were taken without her permission by doctors at Johns Hopkins Hospital in 1951 while she battled cervical cancer. The poem also mentions Venus Hottentot (real name, Sarah Baartman) a Khoekhoe woman who was exhibited in 19th century Europe.

"How to Cry Without Tears" was inspired by Alvin Ailey's ballet "Cry".

"Exhibit D – Dem Dark Bones" is a Duplex after poet Jericho Brown.

"And You Don't Stop" borrows its title from the Sugar Hill Gang's iconic "Rappers Delight" lyrics.

"Intensive Care Rebellion," mentions Crispus Attucks, an African American and Indigenous sailor killed during the Boston Massacre. He was believed to be the first casualty during the American Revolution.

"Sounder, 1972" was taken from an American movie starring Paul Winfield and Cicely Tyson.

Acknowledgements

Many thanks to the editors and staff of the following journals in which these poems first appeared.

African-American Review (Spring/Summer 2023):
"Definition of Blue"
"Emancipation Blues"
"Heartache Ghazal"
"How to Cry Without Tears"
"Kind of Blue: Variation Two"
"Root of My Blues"

Bellevue Literary Review (September 2022):
"How to Shield a Dark Body"

Beloit Poetry Journal (Spring 2020):
"After the Diagnosis"
"Burnt Orange Mountain"
"fragment (n)"
"fragment (v)"
"Kind of Blue: Variation One"
"Q&A"

Boston Review (June 2021):
"Healing"
"Fugitivity" 2nd Prize Winner of the Annual Poetry Prize judged by Sonia Sanchez

Green Mountains Review (August 2021):
"Call and Response"

Interim (December 2020):
"Afro Beautiful"
"A Song for You"
"Self-Portrait as Hoodie"

Interim (November 2021):
"Husband's Instructions"
"Oncology Elegy"
"Revolutionary Fragments"

Obsidian – 50th Annivesary Special Issue (Winter 2025)

"Way in the Middle of the Air"
"Instructions for Intimacy after your Partner's
Cancer Treatment"

Painted Bride Quarterly (January 2024):
"The House that was my Husband's Body"

Prairie Schooner (Winter 2022):
"The House that was my Husband's Body"

Quarterly West (January 2022):
"A-Fib or Revolution Redux"

NAACP Winning Anthology, *This is the Honey* (February 2024)
"Healing"

I owe my life to my fearless mother, Delores Campbell, who loved and never gave up on me, even when it was hard! You are my rock and my role model. Thank you to my brother, Commodore Stewart, for fiercely believing in me. You have been unwavering in your love and your support. We share a brotherly and sisterly bond that will never be broken! Thank you to my beloved father, Roscoe Richard Stewart.

What a blessing you are Rebecca Seiferle! Thank you for helping me give birth to these powerful and necessary poems. Your "Poetic Sequence" workshop unleashed a creative fi-yah in me that brought all the smoke to the pages of this collection.

To the Amazing Ashley M. Jones! I'm deeply honored that you connected with *black frag/ments* and selected it for Hub City Press's inaugural BIPOC Reader Series Prize. Muah!

Thank you, Meg Reid, Kate McMullen, and the staff at Hub City Press for your ongoing support that has brought *black frag/ments* into the world. Thank you for creating the BIPOC Poetry Series and supporting Southern Writers of Color. It's amazing to be part of a press that advocates for its authors.

I love you, Chris Watts! Thank you for keeping the promise you made to me 10 years earlier! Thank you for championing my creative vision and designing a beautiful book cover that speaks to resistance, resilience, and hope. I am forever grateful for your friendship and artistic kinship.

Thank you Tara Betts, Michael Mckeon Bondhus, Jessica Jacobs, Jae Nichelle, and Sara Rose Nordgren who carefully read these poems and gifted me with your brilliance and feedback.

Special thanks to my bestie, Cheryl Whitehead, who read these poems in their early, most vulnerable stages and supports me every step of the way in all of my artistic endeavors. I love you, Chief!

To Phyllis Washington, my African American literature teacher, who is no longer with us. I love you dearly. Thank you for recognizing my talent and stoking my creative flames.

Shout out to Richard Blanco, Terrance Hayes, Sara Rose Nordgren, avery r. young, and Felicia Zamora who showed up and showed out with phenomenal blurbs for *black frag/ments.* Pa-lease know how much I appreciate you all!

Endless gratitude to my many poetry workshop leaders and mentors: Elizabeth Alexander, Tara Betts, Richard Blanco, Tiana Clark, Cyrus Cassells, Toi Derricotte, Cornelius Eady, Nikky Finney, Terrance Hayes, Erica Hunt, Angela Jackson, Heather McHugh, Harryette Mullen, Sara Rose Nordgren, Matthew Olzmann, Tim Seibles, Rebecca Seiferle, Patricia Smith, and Tracy K. Smith.

Huge thanks to the poets who lifted these poems up in workshop and graciously offered feedback including, Tim Berger, Shelly Cato, Rocio Franco, Whitley French, Rebecca Griswold, Gentry Holbert, Quinn Lewis, Kay Moore, Yvette R. Murray, DeAnna Pedigo, Matt Rader, Elizabeth Savage, Zuggie Tate, Kurt Trzcinki, Cheryl Whitehead, Shannon K. Winston, and Trish Woolwine.

Shout out to my beloved Cave Canem poets in Groups A,

E, and B, as well as Dante Micheaux, Nikia Chaney, Cynthia Manick, and Pamela Taylor. Thank you for providing me with a community in a solitary writing world.

L. Lamar Wilson, I am honored to call you my friend and kin bound by love! Thank you for your love, prayers, counsel, and endless support.

Tracy Jones, you are my selfless sister who stands by me no matter what. Thank you so much for your love, advice, and support during our cancer journey and beyond!

Deep love for our family. Kierra White-Rojas, you are our go to—our ride or die! Thank you for your love and strength. Thank you, Ellen Arthur, Steve Brown, Sean Brown, Jaleesa Brown, Krystina Brown, Kathi Cameron, William Cameron, BJ Cameron, Camryn Rojas, Brooklyn Rojas, Frank 'Cisco' Rojas, Miriam Stewart, Ashlei White, Hayward White, and Timothy White, for rallying around us and lending love and support during Reggie's cancer treatment.

Thank you, Sylvia White, for the afternoons you kept Lola while Reggie was in chemotherapy.

Shout out to Chester Fair and Marvin Hudson, for your love and friendship.

To my prayer warriors Bernie Bien-Aime and Theresa Dixon! God and the ancestors heard you all and acted on our behalf.

Extra special thanks to David Jones for holding down the fort at work and to Principal Sharon Johnson for giving me the ability to come and go as needed. Thank you, Diane Fernandez, for picking Lola up from school on those

Wednesdays when I couldn't get there. You are God sent!

To my Miami tribe working diligently to keep the arts alive in our community. I am in the fight with you Beth Boone, Deborah Briggs, Carey Brianna-Hart, Toddra Brunson, Joel Castillo, Ariel Cipolla, Victoria Collado, Christopher Anthony Ferrer, Sefanja Richard Galon, Vanessa Garcia, William Hector, Margaret Ledford, Ivan Lopez, Gladys Ramirez, Vaughn-Rian St. James, Enrique 'Rick' Velez, Hattie Mae Williams and all the other incredibly talented artists on the front lines!

I am grateful to the organizations that provided me creative time, support, and space to write over the years: Atlantic Center for the Arts, Betsy Hotel Writer's Room, Callaloo Creative Writers Workshop, Cave Canem, City Theatre Miami, Coconut Grove Theatre Festival, Fine Arts Work Center, Miami Light Project, Palm Beach Poetry Festival, Sewanee School of Letters, SWWIM, and the Watering Hole.

To God and the ancestors, only you know what our family went through. There were so many dark days when I cried out to you from sterile rooms. I could feel your presence. It was your grace and mercy that brought us through. Thank you!

Finally, to the reader who holds this book in their hands. I give this to you with joy!

PUBLISHING
New & Extraordinary
VOICES FROM THE
AMERICAN SOUTH

HUB CITY PRESS is a non-profit independent press in Spartanburg, SC that publishes well-crafted, high-quality works by new and established authors, with an emphasis on the Southern experience. We are committed to high-caliber novels, short stories, poetry, plays, memoir, and works emphasizing regional culture and history. We are particularly interested in books with a strong sense of place.

Hub City Press is an imprint of the non-profit Hub City Writers Project, founded in 1995 to foster a sense of community through the literary arts. Our metaphor of organization purposely looks backward to the nineteenth century when Spartanburg was known as the "hub city," a place where railroads converged and departed.

The Hub City Press BIPOC Poetry Series was created to spotlight poetry by writers working in the American South, writing about BIPOC communities. Two finalists were selected by Editor-at-Large Ashley M. Jones.The Hub City Press BIPOC Poetry Series is open to poets of all stages of their careers who reside in or are from the South and self-identify as a member of a Southern BIPOC community. This series is made possible with funding from the Poetry Foundation.

BIPOC PRIZE HONOREES

2025: *the past is a jean jacket* cloud delfina cardona

2026: *black frag/ments* Lolita Stewart-White